to d...   ...sa...
on...

Love
    Gene and Brenda

THE NO GOOD DIRTY ROTTEN LOW DOWN

Book of Love

THE NO GOOD GOOD DIRTY ROTTEN LOW DOWN

Book of

Love

With an introduction by E. Jean Carroll
Advice Columnist ELLE Magazine

Compiled by Eileen Bertelli

NO GOOD BOOKS

Published by NoGoodBooks,
an imprint of 1500 Books, LLC, Warwick, NY

www.NoGoodBooks.com

Printed in the United States of America

ISBN 13: 978-1933698-20-5

Design by Sandra Correa
Vertigo Design Studios, www.vdsny.com

Grateful Thanks

to
E. Jean Carroll
and to
Anastasia Miller.
Your contributions are, well, priceless.

And so to my favorite happy-go-lucky-Scot...

you be the best baby!

❦♡❦ Introduction ❦♡❦

Hello there!

I see you're about to begin reading *The No Good Dirty Rotten Low Down Book of Love*. Excellent. It's a very witty collection—some damn funny stuff. Kick off your shoes, pour yourself a vodka, put your feet up on the cushion— oh. You like reading in the car? Well, sure. There's no law against reading in the car. Make yourself comfortable. Got a snack? Ah! Delightful! A whole chocolate cake to yourself! Good. That's right, go ahead. You don't even *need* a fork.

Relax. Read. Disconnect from the world.

Uh, shouldn't you turn off your iPhone?

You don't want to be disturbed while reading this dazzling new book, do you? Oh? You *do* want to be disturbed? Oh, well, and how many texts have you sent this person?

Ah.

That's a lot of texts.

No, I will *not* take your picture with your iPhone. No. I'm here to introduce the book. I'm here to tell you *The No Good Dirty Rotten Low Down Book of Love* is a wild ride through the deranged world of love. I'm here to tell you I'm an authority on love because I write the "Ask E. Jean" column, the longest running advice column in American publishing, and, hunny, this book describes the brutal truth.

Pardon me?

No. I will not shoot you. I don't care if you are the "poster child" for *The No Good Dirty Rotten Low Down Book of Love*. You will have to hold the iPhone out and shoot yourself—that's right. Smile.

Oh!

Very saucy!—wait. What are you doing? OH! MY! Uh—I, uh, uh, uh, I don't, uh, advise you to remove any MORE garments, seriously. If you want to sit here taking naked pictures of yourself and e-mailing them to your ex, go ahead. But, really, you don't know what you're missing with the brilliant *The No Good Dirty Rotten Low Down Book of Love*. That's right. Put your sweater back on. Good. You want to know something? Listen:

I'm proud of you.

Yes, I am. I'm proud of you for *buying* this entertaining book about how love can rip you to shreds. It shows that you still have a huge capacity for being ironic and clever. Wait, where are you going?

Oh!

I didn't realize you're parked in *front* of your ex-lover's house. Oh dear. I strongly, strongly urge you to stay in the car. OK, I strongly urge you to get *back* in the car. I don't think your ex will like the—watch out for the azaleas! Uh, well . . . no, actually . . . I'm not sure if *The No Good Dirty Rotten Low Down Book of Love* is heavy enough to break a window. I know it's the smartest book about love I've seen in years, but I'm not quite certain if it weighs enough to break that—

Ruuuuuuuuuuuuuunnnnnn!!

Start the engine!

What's this?

Oh, I see you have another copy of the book. Excellent! No doubt, as Oscar Wilde said, you "have many other calls of a similar character to make in the neighborhood."

E. Jean Carroll
Advice Columnist
ELLE Magazine

Everyone admits that love
is wonderful and necessary,
yet no one agrees on just what it is.

Diane Ackerman

At First Blush…

How on earth are you ever going to explain
in terms of chemistry and physics
so important a biological phenomenon
as first love?

Albert Einstein

I was nauseous and tingly all over.
I was either in love or I had smallpox.

Woody Allen

It's easy to fall in love.
The hard part is finding someone
to catch you.

Bertrand Russell

First love is a little foolish
and a lot of curiosity.

George Bernard Shaw

Love is the strange bewilderment
which overtakes one person
on account of another person.

James Thurber

Love, to the outside observer,
is often mistaken for lunacy.

Les Vierges (The Virgins)

One's first love is always perfect
until one meets one's second love.

Elizabeth Aston

First love is a kind of vaccination
which saves a man
from catching the complaint
the second time.

Honoré de Balzac

We always believe our first love is our last,
and our last love our first.

George John Whyte-Melville

First love, with its frantic
haughty imagination,
swings its object clear
of the everyday,
over the rut of living,
making him all looks,
silences, gestures, attitudes,
a burning phrase with no context.

Elizabeth Bowen

And how can that be true love
which is falsely attempted?
Love is a familiar; Love is a devil:
there is no evil angel but Love.

William Shakespeare

A man always remembers his first love
with special tenderness,
but after that
he begins to bunch them.

H.L. Mencken

The magic of first love
is our ignorance that it can never end.

Benjamin Disraeli

He who loves thinks
that the others are blind;
the others think that
he is crazy.

Arabian Proverb

Head Over Heels...

Love is a fire.
But whether it is going to
warm your heart
or burn down your house,
you can never tell.

Joan Crawford

We don't believe
in rheumatism and true love
until after the first attack.

Marie E. von Eschenbach

If love is so important to have
that one doesn't want to lose it,
why is it when we find true love
we often don't notice it?

Anonymous

I can see from your utter misery,
from your eagerness
to misunderstand each other,
and from your thoroughly bad temper,
that this is the real thing.

Peter Ustinov

True love comes quietly,
without banners or flashing lights.
If you hear bells,
get your ears checked.

Erich Segal

If only one could tell true love from false love
as one can tell mushrooms from toadstools.

Katherine Mansfield

You say that love is nonsense....
I tell you it is no such thing.
For weeks and months it is a steady physical pain,
an ache about the heart,
never leaving one, by night or by day;
a long strain on one's nerves
like toothache or rheumatism,
not intolerable at any one instant,
but exhausting by its
steady drain on the strength.

Henry Brooks Adams

True love is like ghosts,
which everybody talks about
and few have seen.

François de La Rochefoucauld

And what's romance?
Usually, a nice little tale
where you have everything
As You Like It,
where rain never wets your jacket
and gnats never bite your nose
and it's always daisy-time.

D. H. Lawrence

People in love, it is well known,
suffer extreme conceptual delusions;
the most common of these being
that other people find your condition
as thrilling and eye-watering
as you do yourselves.

Julian Barnes

The essence of romantic love
is that wonderful beginning,
after which sadness and impossibility
may become the rule.

Anita Brookner

They say true love
only comes around once
and you have to hold out
and be strong until then.
I have been waiting.
I have been searching.

Henry Rollins

Love is blind, so you have to feel your way.

Brazilian Proverb

This Way Lies Madness…

When love is not madness,
it is not love.

Pedro Calderón de la Barca

We always deceive ourselves
twice about the people we love—
first to their advantage,
then to their disadvantage.

Albert Camus

Reason and love are sworn enemies.

Pierre Corneille

In a great romance,
each person basically plays a part
that the other really likes.

Elizabeth Ashley

Love without reason
lasts the longest.

Jean-François Regnard

Love can sometimes be magic.
But magic can sometimes...
just be an illusion.

Javan

Romantic love
is mental illness.
But it's a pleasurable one.
It's a drug.
It distorts reality,
and that's the point of it.
It would be impossible
to fall in love
with someone
that you really saw.

Fran Lebowitz

Whatever deceives men
seems to produce
a magical enchantment.

Plato

The happiest liaisons
are based
on mutual misunderstanding.

François de La Rochefoucauld

A person needs a little madness,
or else they never dare cut the rope and be free.

Nikos Kazantzakis

Love is a game
of secret, cunning stratagems,
in which only the fools
who are fated to lose
reveal their true aims or motives—
even to themselves.

Eugene O'Neill

I like someone who is a little crazy
but coming from a good place.
I think scars are sexy because it means
you made a mistake that led to a mess.

Angelina Jolie

For you to ask advice
on the rules of love
is no better than to
ask advice on the
rules of madness.

Terence

If this be not love, it is madness,
and then it is pardonable.

William Congreve

Love is like pi—
natural, irrational, and very important.

Lisa Hoffman

You may be right I may be crazy
But it just may be a lunatic you're looking for.

Billy Joel, You May Be Right

When one is in love,
one always begins
by deceiving oneself,
and one always ends
by deceiving others.
That is what the world calls
a romance.

Oscar Wilde

Hatred is the madness of the heart.

Lord Byron

Lovers always think
that other people are blind.

Spanish Proverb

I'll Know It
When I See It...

Sex without love
is merely healthy exercise.

Robert Heinlein

Love is not the dying moan
of a distant violin—
it's the triumphant twang
of a bedspring.

S.J. Perelman

Sex is emotion in motion.

Mae West

Love ain't nothing but sex misspelled.

Harlan Ellison

A man must be potent and orgasmic
to ensure the future of the race.
A woman only needs to be available.

William H. Masters & Virginia E. Johnson

Sex is a bad thing
because
it rumples the clothes.

Jacqueline Kennedy Onassis

Love is the self-delusion
we manufacture
to justify the trouble we take
to have sex.

Dan Greenburg

Nothing makes you forget about love
like sex.

Staci Beasley

There is nothing safe about sex.
There never will be.

Norman Mailer

Sex relieves tension—love causes it.

Woody Allen

I wouldn't recommend
sex, drugs or insanity
for everyone,
but they've always
worked for me.

Hunter S. Thompson

Sex is a momentary itch,
love never lets you go.

Kingsley Amis

Sex is funny and love is serious.

Stephan Jenkins

There will be sex after death,
we just won't be able to feel it.

Lily Tomlin

Bed is the poor man's opera.

Italian Proverb

Time Flies When You're Having Fun...

Love makes the time pass.
Time makes love pass.

Euripides

Love is the flower of life,
and blossoms unexpectedly and without law,
and must be plucked where it is found,
and enjoyed for the brief hour of its duration.

D.H. Lawrence

The only difference
between friends and lovers
is about four minutes.

Scott Roeben

Pleasure of love lasts but a moment,
Pain of love lasts a lifetime.

Bette Davis

I've been told when you meet the right person
you know immediately.
How come when you meet the wrong person
it takes a year-and-a-half?

Phil Hanley

One should always be wary
of anyone who promises that their love
will last longer than a weekend.

Quentin Crisp

Love with passion but only for a few minutes.

Ninon de Lenclos

Time is too slow
for those who wait,
too swift for those who fear,
too long for those who grieve,
too short for those who rejoice,
but for those who love,
time is eternity.

Henry Van Dyke

When you're in love it's the most glorious
two-and-a-half days of your life.

Richard Lewis

There is a time for work.
And a time for love.
That leaves no other time.

Coco Chanel

When you are courting a nice girl
an hour seems like a second.
When you sit on a red-hot cinder
a second seems like an hour.
That's relativity.

Albert Einstein

We waste time looking for the perfect lover
instead of creating the perfect love.

Tom Robbins

Love vanquishes time.
To lovers, a moment can be eternity,
eternity can be the tick of a clock.

Mary Parrish

Time, ain't nothin, but time.
It's a verse with no rhyme,
Man, it all comes down to you.

Bon Jovi, Next 100 Years

It is better to be without a wife
for a minute
than without tobacco
for an hour.

Estonian Proverb

Best Friends Forever?

Nothing takes the taste out of peanut butter
quite like unrequited love.

Charles M. Schulz

The best love affairs are
those we never had.

Norman Lindsay

You love me so much,
you want to put me in your pocket.
And I should die there smothered.

D. H. Lawrence

The love that lasts the longest
is the love that is never returned.

W. Somerset Maugham

How many young men,
in all previous times
of unprecedented steadiness,
had turned suddenly wild and wicked
for the same reason, and,
in an ecstasy of unrequited love,
taken to wrench off door-knockers,
and invert the boxes
of rheumatic watchmen!

Charles Dickens

All love is unrequited. All of it.

J. Michael Straczynski

Love, unrequited, robs me of my rest:
Love, hopeless love, my ardent soul encumbers:
Love, nightmare-like, lies heavy on my chest,
And weaves itself into my midnight slumbers!

William S. Gilbert

Let no one who loves
be called unhappy.
Even love unreturned
has its rainbow.

J. M. Barrie

If I love you,
what business is it of yours?

Johann Wolfgang von Goethe

A mighty pain to love it is,
and 'tis a pain that pain to miss;
but of all the pains, the greatest pain is to love,
but love in vain.

Abraham Crowley

To love someone
who does not love you,
is like shaking a tree
to make the dew drops fall.

Congolese Proverb

That Which Does Not Kill You...

We say we love flowers,
yet we pluck them.
We say we love trees,
yet we cut them down.
And people still wonder why
some are afraid when told
they are loved.

Anonymous

Love does not begin and end
the way we seem to think it does.
Love is a battle, love is a war;
love is a growing up.

James Baldwin

It is explained that all relationships
require a little give and take.
This is untrue.
Any partnership demands
that we give and give and give
and at the last,
as we flop into our graves exhausted,
we are told that we didn't give enough.

Quentin Crisp

One does not love a place the less for having
suffered in it
unless it has all been suffering,
nothing but suffering.

Jane Austen

Can there be a love which does not
make demands on its object?

Confucius

Reserve delicacy of sentiment
for friendship;
accept love for what it is….
The more dignity you give it,
the more dangerous you make it.

Ninon de Lenclos

Love is a sort of hostile transaction,
very necessary to keep the world going,
but by no means a sinecure to
the parties concerned.

Lord Byron

Love is a perky elf
dancing a merry little jig
and then suddenly
he turns on you
with a miniature machine-gun.

Matt Groening

Love is a smoke
made with the fume of sighs.
Being purged, a fire sparkling in lovers' eyes.
Being vexed, a sea nourished with lovers' tears.
What is it else?
A madness most discreet,
a choking gall and a preserving sweet.

William Shakespeare

Love is like the truth,
sometimes it prevails,
sometimes it hurts.

Victor M. Garcia, Jr.

To love and win is the best thing.
To love and lose, the next best.

William M. Thackeray

Gravitation can not
be held responsible
for people falling in love.

Albert Einstein

Maybe love is like luck.
You have to go all the way to find it.

Robert Mitchum

In reality,
in love there is a permanent suffering
which joy neutralizes,
renders virtual, delays,
but which can at any moment become
what it would have become long earlier
if one had not obtained what one wanted,
atrocious.

Marcel Proust

Love involves a peculiar unfathomable
combination of understanding
and misunderstanding.

Diane Arbus

The one who loves you
will also make you weep.

Argentine Proverb

What Now, My Love?

The greater your capacity to love,
the greater your capacity
to feel the pain.

Jennifer Aniston

Have you ever been in love? Horrible isn't it?...
Love takes hostages. It gets inside you.
It eats you out and leaves you
crying in the darkness....
It hurts. Not just in the imagination.
Not just in the mind.
It's a soul-hurt, a real
gets-inside-you-
and-rips-you-apart pain.
I hate love.

Neil Gaiman

Love is more pleasant
once you get out of your twenties.
It doesn't hurt all the time.

Andy A. Rooney

Love is an exploding cigar
we willingly smoke.

Lynda Barry

Love is an incurable malady
like those pathetic states
in which rheumatism affords the sufferer
a brief respite only to be replaced
by epileptiform headaches.

Marcel Proust

Love is a universal migraine,
A bright stain on the vision
Blotting out reason.

Robert Graves

Why love if losing hurts so much?
I have no answers anymore;
only the life I have lived.
The pain now is part
of the happiness then.

Anthony Hopkins

He who has been smitten by the arrows of love
never again fears any other wound.

Anonymous

To love is to suffer.
To avoid suffering one must not love.
But then one suffers from not loving.
Therefore to love is to suffer,
not to love is to suffer. To suffer is to suffer.
To be happy is to love.
To be happy then is to suffer.
But suffering makes one unhappy.
Therefore, to be unhappy
one must love, or love to suffer,
or suffer from too much happiness.
I hope you're getting this down.

Woody Allen

The pain of love is the pain of being alive.
It is a perpetual wound.

Maureen Duffy

I walked under a bus,
I got hit by a train.
I keep falling in love,
which is kinda the same.

Bachelor Girl, Buses And Trains

Loving,
knowing that you are going to get hurt,
is like living knowing
that you are going to die.
But not loving so you don't get hurt,
is like killing yourself
before you die.

Anonymous

Dogs love their friends
and bite their enemies,
quite unlike people,
who are incapable
of pure love and
always have to
mix love and hate.

Sigmund Freud

I met a young man
who was wounded in love,
I met another man
who was wounded in hatred.

Bob Dylan, A Hard Rain's A-Gonna Fall

People talk about how great love is,
but that's bullshit.
Love hurts.
Feelings are disturbing.
People are taught that pain
is evil and dangerous.
How can they deal with love
if they're afraid to feel?
Pain is meant to wake us up.

Jim Morrison

Scratch a lover and find an enemy.

German Proverb

S/he Loves Me;
S/he Loves Me Not…

The hottest love has the coldest end.

Socrates

Love is like pizza—
when it's good, it's really good.
When it's bad,
it's still pretty good.

Anonymous

We perceive
when love begins
and when it declines
by our embarrassment
when alone together.

La Bruyère

Parting is all we know of heaven
and all we need of hell.

Emily Dickinson

He was my North, my South, my East and West,
My working week and Sunday rest,
My noon, my midnight, my talk, my song;
I thought that love would last forever:
I was wrong.

W.H. Auden

The heaviest object in the world
is the body of the woman
you have ceased to love

Maxim Luc de Clapier, Marquis de Vauvenargues

I make you laugh and you make me cry,
I believe it's time for me to fly.

REO Speedwagon, Time for Me to Fly

Romantic love is an illusion.
Most of us discover this truth
at the end of a love affair
or else when the
sweet emotions of love
lead us into marriage
and then turn down their flames.

Thomas Moore

Oh, life is a glorious cycle of song,
A medley of extemporanea;
And love is a thing that can never go wrong;
And I am Marie of Roumania.

Dorothy Parker

People change and forget to tell each other.

Lillian Hellman

Hearts, like thieves,
never give back lost things.

Guatemalan Proverb

Can't We All Just
Get Along?

Most things break, including hearts.
The lessons of life amount not to wisdom,
but to scar tissue and callus.

Wallace Stegner

Hit me with a shovel,
because I can't believe I dug you.

Skid Row, Creep Show

Hate leaves ugly scars,
love leaves beautiful ones.

Mignon McLaughlin

If we judge of love by its usual effects,
it resembles hatred more than friendship.

François de La Rochefoucauld

'Tis an old tale, and often told;
But did my fate and wish agree,
Ne'er had been read, in story old,
Of maiden true betray'd for gold,
That loved, or was avenged, like me!

Sir Walter Scott

Nothing ends nicely, that's why it ends.

Tom Cruise

I will not leave you
until I have seen you hanged.

Molière

No more tears now;
I will think about revenge.

Mary, Queen of Scots

All the old knives
That have rusted in my back,
I drive in yours.

Phaedrus

If to know you is to hate you,
then loving you must be like suicide.

Green Day, Jackass

Love is the big booming beat
which covers up the noise of hate.

Margaret Cho

Those who love you will make you weep;
those who hate you will make you laugh.

Russian Proverb

The War Between
The Sexes…

Women were created
to drive men crazy.
Whether it's crazy
in a good way,
or a bad way,
is the question.

Les Vierges (The Virgins)

What would men be
without women?
Scarce, sir, mighty scarce.

Mark Twain

Great men are not always idiots.

Karen Elizabeth Gordon

Women are like elephants.
Everyone likes to look at them
but no-one likes to have to keep one.

W.C. Fields

Love is the delusion
that one woman
differs from another.

H.L. Mencken

Ah, women.
They make the highs higher
and the lows more frequent.

Friedrich Wilhelm Nietzsche

Thou art to me a delicious torment.

Ralph Waldo Emerson

A woman occasionally
is quite a serviceable substitute
for masturbation.

Karl Kraus

The more boys I meet
the more I love my dog.

Carrie Underwood, The More Boys I Meet

There's a great woman behind every idiot.

John Lennon

As far as I'm concerned,
being any gender is a drag.

Patti Smith

The little rift between the sexes
is astonishingly widened
by simply teaching
one set of catchwords
to the girls and another to the boys.

Robert Louis Stevenson

What a strange thing man is;
and what a stranger thing woman.

Lord Byron

Of all the animals,
the boy is the most unmanageable.

Plato

Mountains appear more lofty
the nearer they are approached,
but great men resemble them not
in this particular.

Lady Marguerite Blessington

The greatest love is a mother's,
then a dog's,
then a sweetheart's.

Polish Proverb

Change Of Heart...

The heart was made to be broken.

Oscar Wilde

If all hearts were open
and all desires known—
as they would be
if people showed their souls—
how many gapings, sighings,
clenched fists, knotted brows,
broad grins, and red eyes
should we see in the market-place!

Thomas Hardy

You don't die of a broken heart,
you only wish you did.

Marilyn Peterson

Your heart is my piñata.

Chuck Palahniuk

You can lead a heart to love,
but you can't make it fall.

Johnny McRae & Steve Clark,
You Can't Make A Heart Love Somebody

There are two tragedies in life.
One is to lose your heart's desire.
The other is to gain it.

George Bernard Shaw

Broken hearts die slowly.

Langston Hughes

Once a woman has given you her heart,
you can never get rid of the rest of her.

Sir John Vanbrugh

I prithee send me back my heart,
Since I cannot have thine;
For if from yours you will not part,
Why, then, shouldst thou have mine?

John Suckling

The heart is the only broken instrument
that works.

T.E. Kalem

The logic of the heart is absurd.

Julie de Lespinasse

When your heart is broken,
your boats are burned:
nothing matters any more.
It is the end of happiness
and the beginning of peace.

George Bernard Shaw

Though talking face to face,
their hearts are a thousand miles apart.

Chinese Proverb

Made In Heaven...

The war between the sexes
is the only one in which
both sides regularly
sleep with the enemy.

Quentin Crisp

Sometimes I wonder if men and women
really suit each other.
Perhaps they should live next door,
and just visit now and then.

Katharine Hepburn

If two people love each other,
there can be no happy end to it.

Ernest Hemingway

What is irritating about love
is that it is a crime
that requires an accomplice.

Charles Baudelaire

There are women who do not like
to cause suffering to many men at a time,
and who prefer to concentrate on one man:
These are the faithful women.

Alfred Capus

One half of the world cannot understand
the pleasures of the other.

Jane Austen

Love is a narcissism shared by two.

Rita Mae Brown

When two people are under the influence
of the most violent, most insane, most delusive,
and most transient of passions,
they are required to swear that they will
remain in that excited, abnormal, and
exhausting condition continuously
until death do them part.

George Bernard Shaw

Love and dignity cannot share
the same abode.

Ovid

The concept of two people
living together for 25 years
without a serious dispute
suggests a lack of spirit
only to be admired in sheep.

A.P. Herbert

Love is like the measles;
we all have to go through it.

Jerome K. Jerome

It destroys one's nerves
to be amiable every day
to the same human being.

Benjamin Disraeli

The most important thing
in a relationship
between a man and a woman
is that one of them be good at taking orders.

Linda Festa

Love is the gross exaggeration
of the difference between
one person and everyone else.

George Bernard Shaw

Keep your tents apart
and your hearts together.

Tuareg Proverb

That Old Ball
And Chain...

Love: a temporary insanity,
curable by marriage.

Ambrose Bierce

Getting married is easy.
Staying married is more difficult.
Staying happily married for a lifetime
should rank among the fine arts.

Attributed to Roberta Flack

Marriage is the triumph of imagination
over intelligence.

Oscar Wilde

All marriages are happy.
It's trying to live together afterwards
that causes all the problems.

Shelley Winters

I love being married.
It's so great to find that one
special person you want
to annoy for the rest of your life.

Rita Rudner

Marriage is like twirling a baton,
turning handsprings or eating with chopsticks.
It looks easy until you try it.

Helen Rowland

Brought up to respect the conventions,
love had to end in marriage.
I'm afraid it did.

Bette Davis

If variety is the spice of life,
marriage is the
big can of leftover Spam.

Johnny Carson

If we take matrimony at its lowest,
we regard it as a sort of friendship
recognised by the police.

Robert Louis Stevenson

Nothing anybody tells you about marriage helps.

Max Siegel

Whenever a husband and wife
begin to discuss their marriage,
they are giving evidence at an inquest.

H.L. Mencken

I was married by a judge.
I should have asked for a jury.

Groucho Marx

Love is a constant interrogation.

Milan Kundera

One of the aims of connubial bliss
is to punish both parties.

H.L. Mencken

"I am" is reportedly
the shortest sentence
in the English language.
Could it be that "I do"
is the longest sentence?

George Carlin

I first learned the concepts of non-violence
in my marriage.

Mohandas K. Gandhi

Marriage is like putting your hand
into a bag of snakes
in the hope of pulling out an eel.

Leonardo da Vinci

If you want to read about love and marriage
you've got to buy two separate books.

Alan King

The woman who loves her husband
corrects his faults;
the man that loves his wife
exaggerates them.

Armenian Proverb

Lyin' Eyes And
Cheatin' Hearts...

We have to distrust each other.
It is our only defence against betrayal.

Tennessee Williams

A man can have two,
maybe three love affairs
while he's married.
After that it's cheating.

Yves Montand

If you marry a man
who cheats on his wife,
you'll be married to a man
who cheats on his wife.

Ann Landers

It can be great fun
to have an affair
with a bitch.

Louis Auchincloss

Husbands are chiefly good as lovers
when they are betraying their wives.

Marilyn Monroe

Love is a game in which one always cheats.

Honoré de Balzac

Monogamy is the Western custom
of one wife and hardly any mistresses.

H.H. Munro (Saki)

Three things are men most likely
to be cheated in,
a horse, a wig, and a wife.

Benjamin Franklin

Do infants enjoy infancy
as much as
adults enjoy adultery?

Murray Banks

What men call gallantry
and gods adultery
is much more common
where the climate's sultry.

Lord Byron

There were three of us in this marriage,
so it was a bit crowded.

Diana, Princess of Wales

When a man steals your wife
there is no better revenge
than to let him keep her.

Sacha Guitry

An affair now and then
is good for a marriage.
It adds spice,
stops it from getting boring...
I ought to know.

Bette Davis

You know of course
that the Tasmanians,
who never committed adultery,
are now extinct.

W. Somerset Maugham

The Love Bird
is 100% faithful to his mate,
as long as they are
locked together in the same cage.

Will Cuppy

Wars are caused by women and priests.

Czech Proverb

The Fat Lady Sings…

A wife lasts only
for the length of the marriage,
but an ex-wife
is there for the rest of your life.

Jim Samuels

Whenever I date a guy,
I think, is this the man I want my children
to spend their weekends with?

Rita Rudner

Alimony is like buying oats for a dead horse.

Arthur Baer

Even hooligans marry,
though they know that marriage
is but for a little while.
It is alimony that is forever.

Quentin Crisp

My husband and I have never
considered divorce...
murder sometimes, but never divorce.

Dr. Joyce Brothers

I guess the only way to stop divorce
is to stop marriage.

Will Rogers

My toughest fight was with my first wife.

Muhammad Ali

Being divorced
is like being hit by a Mack truck.
If you live through it,
you start looking very carefully
to the right and to the left.

Jean Kerr

She cried, and the judge wiped her tears
with my checkbook.

Tommy Manville

Just another of our many disagreements.
He wants a no-fault divorce,
whereas I would prefer
to have the bastard crucified.

J.B. Handlesman

You don't know anything about a woman
until you meet her in court.

Norman Mailer

If marriage means you fell in love,
does divorce mean you climbed out?

Anonymous

Divorce is a game played by lawyers.

Cary Grant

The happiest time in any man's life
is just after the first divorce.

John Kenneth Galbraith

It wasn't exactly a divorce—I was traded.

Tim Conway

When a neighbor gets divorced
everyone thinks of his own wife.

Swiss Proverb

I Want To Be Alone...

It's better to be unhappy alone
than unhappy with someone.

Marilyn Monroe

One of the advantages
of living alone
is that you don't
have to wake up
in the arms of a loved one.

Marion Smith

Stay with me, I want to be alone.

Attributed to Joey Adams

It is unpleasant to go alone,
even to be drowned.

Russian Proverb

The dread of loneliness
is greater than the fear of bondage,
so we get married.

Cyril Connelly

It may be quieter to sleep alone,
but not warmer.

Italian Proverb

It is more fun contemplating
somebody else's navel than your own.

Attributed to Arthur Hoppe

Him that I love,
I wish to be free—
even from me.

Anne Morrow Lindbergh

Eagles we see fly alone;
and they are but sheep
which always herd together.

Sir Philip Sidney

One can acquire everything in solitude
but character.

Marie Stendhal

People drain me,
even the closest of friends,
and I find loneliness to be
the best state in the union
to live in.

Margaret Cho

Better alone than in bad company.

French Proverb

Is The Second Time
The Charm?

A second marriage is
the triumph of hope over experience.

Samuel Johnson

"Two mothers-in-law."
Lord John Russell

*On being asked what he would consider
a proper punishment for bigamy.*

So heavy is the chain of wedlock
that it needs two to carry it,
and sometimes three.

Alexandre Dumas

One man's folly is another man's wife.

Helen Rowland

Love is lovelier, the second time around
Just as wonderful, with both feet on the ground.
It's that second time you hear your love song sung
Makes you think perhaps that love,
like youth, is wasted on the young.

Sammy Cahn & Jimmy Van Heusen,
The Second Time Around

There is so little difference between husbands
you might as well keep the first.

Adela Rogers St. Johns

A proof that experience is of no use,
is that the end of one love
does not prevent us from
beginning another.

Paul Bourget

I've been married to one Marxist
and one Fascist, and neither one
would take the garbage out.

Lee Grant

Bigamy is having one wife too many.
Monogamy is the same.

Oscar Wilde

Many a man owes his success to his first wife
and his second wife to his success.

Jim Backus

I've had bad luck with both my wives.
The first one left me and the second one didn't.

Patrick Murra

Some marriages break up, and some do not,
and in our world you can usually explain
the former better than the latter.

Mignon McLaughlin

The most dangerous food is wedding cake.

American Proverb

**Bad as I like ye,
it's worse without ye.**

Irish Proverb